Don't Cross Your Bridge Before...

...you pay the toll.

by Judith
Frost Stark

PRICE/STERN/SLOAN
Publishers, Inc., Los Angeles
1985

THIRD PRINTING — JULY 1985

Copyright © 1982, 1985 by Judith Frost Stark
Published by Price/Stern/Sloan Publishers, Inc.
410 North La Cienega Boulevard, Los Angeles, California 90048

ISBN: 0-8431-0617-4

Introduction

Judith Frost Stark has been teaching first-graders to read and write English for the past twenty years, a job which she still enjoys. She has developed and used many original teaching ideas as a means of motivating students.

DON'T CROSS YOUR BRIDGE BEFORE... was created from one such idea. Mrs. Stark would begin sentences on paper and leave a blank space for the children to print words which completed the thought. Many of her six-year-old friends even added drawings to the "proverbs." Through the years, Mrs. Stark saved her favorite "priceless proverbs," as she calls them, and gathered a collection for publication.

The book is dedicated to all children everywhere, their mothers and fathers, their grandmothers and grandfathers, their friends and on and on and on.

Don't cross your bridge before you...

pay the toll.

A B C D E F G

People who
live in
glass houses
shouldn't...

O P Q R S T

H I J K L M N

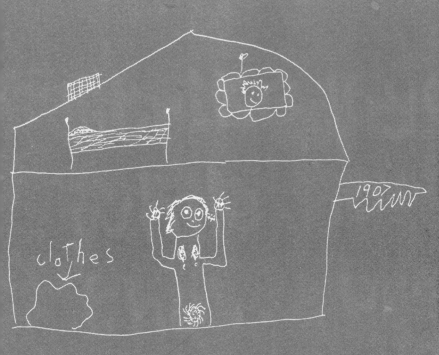

clothes

un dress.

U V W X Y Z

'Tis better

to be safe

than ...

punch a sixth grader.

Strike

while

the...

bug is close

It's always darkest before

daylight savings time .

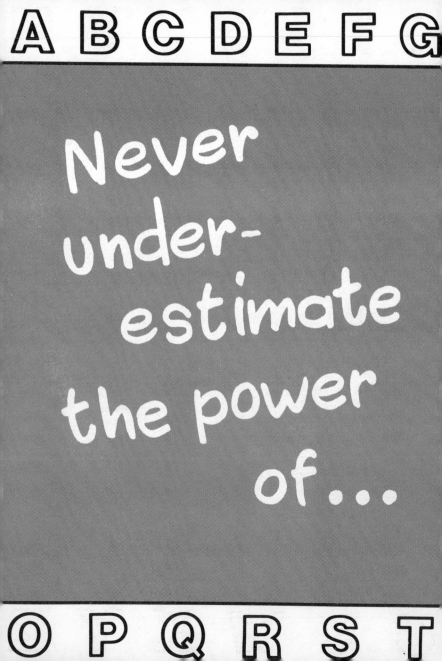

termites.

Still

waters...

will get you nowhere.

You can
lead a
horse to
water,
but...

how ?

Don't bite the hand that...

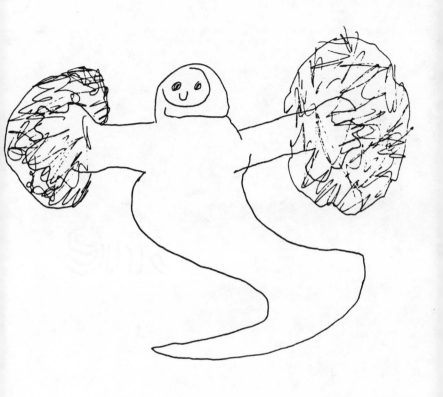

looks dirty .

No
news
is...

San Frinsiko Cronicl

impossible.

A miss is
as good
as a....

Mr. !

If you sing
before

breakfast,
you'll...

have music in your mouth.

You can't teach an old dog new ...

$4 + (5 - 3) = \square$ $9 \times 2 =$

$4 + (4 + 4) = \square$ $12 \times 4 =$

math.

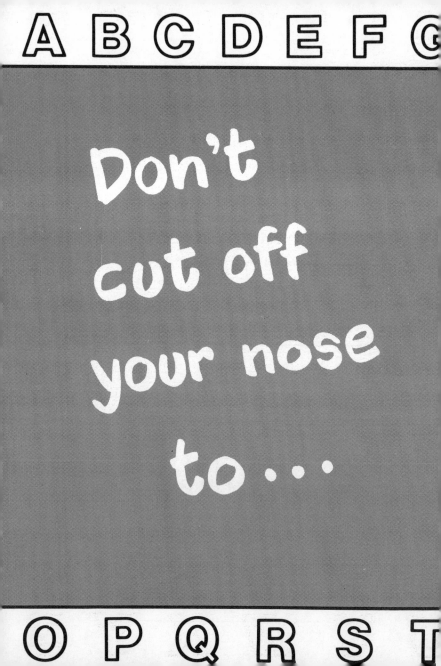

HIJKLMN

get away from the smell.

UVWXYZ

Sticks and stones will break your bones, but...

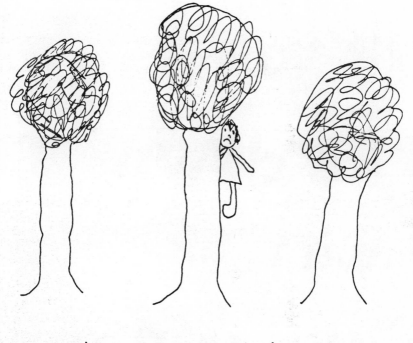

not if you hide.

Low, this is simple.

If you
lie down
with
the dogs...

you'll stink in the morning.

An
idle mind
is...

the best way to relaxs.

A B C D E F G

He who

marries

for money...

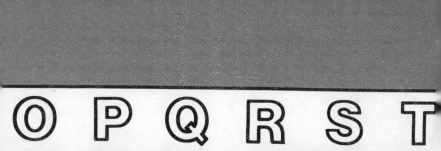

O P Q R S T

better be nice to his wife.

When
the cat's
away...

no pooh!

As you shall make your bed, so shall you...

mess it up.

Happy

the

bride...

Who gets all the presents.

A penny

saved

is...

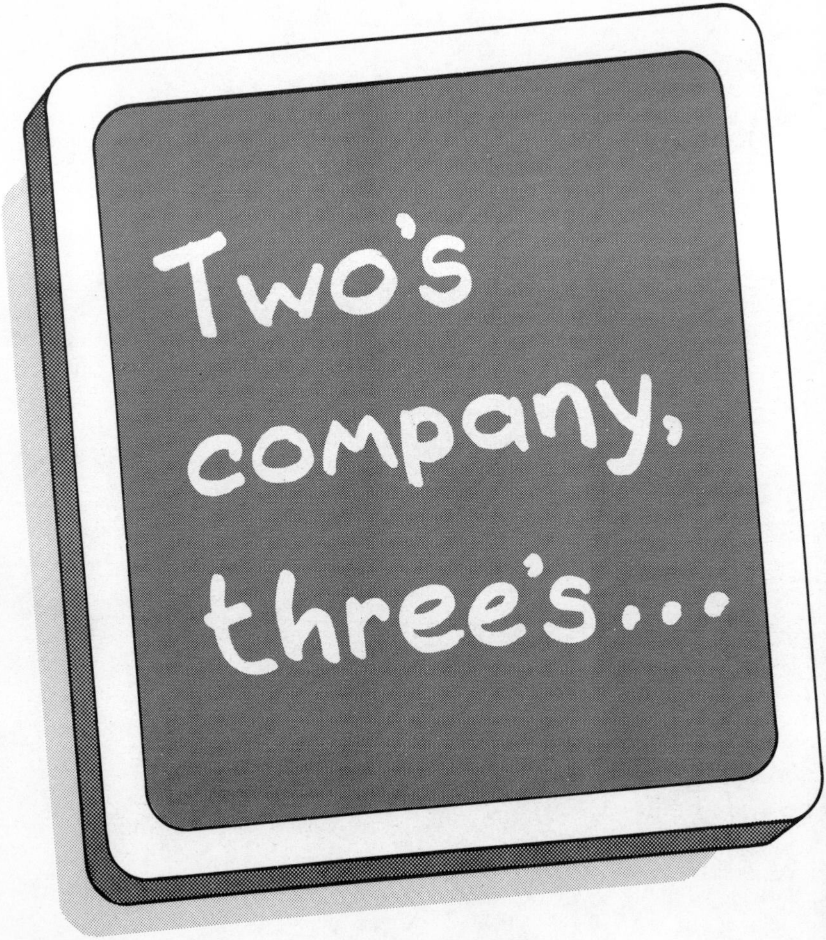
Two's
company,
three's...

the muskateers.

Don't
put off until
tomorrow
what...

you put on to go to bed.

Laugh and the world laughs with you. Cry and...

You have to blow your nose.

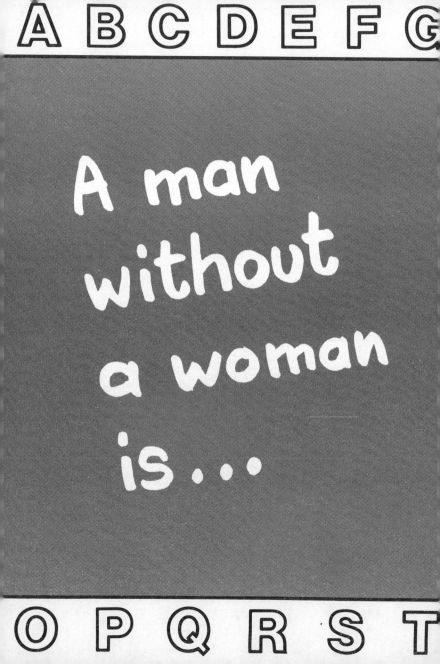

probably poor.

Money is the root of...

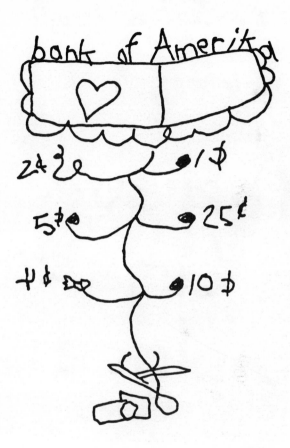

the bank of America.

There's
a time and
a place...

to meet grandma.

What's
good for
the goose
is ...

a gooster.

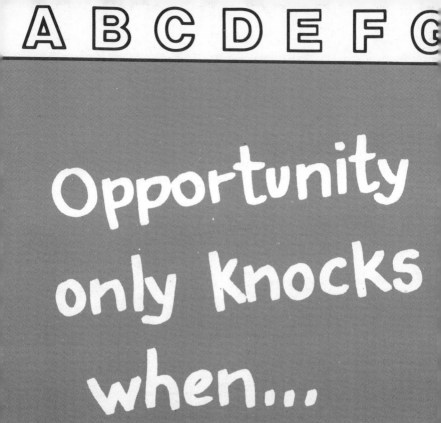

Opportunity only knocks when...

She can't reach the doorbell.

Children
should be
seen
and not....

spanked or grounded.

when
at first
you don't
succeed...

get new batteries.

You get
out of
something
what you...

saw pictured on the box.

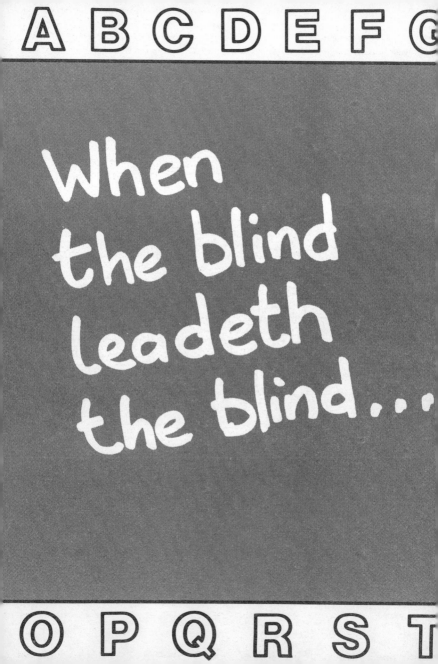

get out of thayr way.

There's
no fool
like...

Aunt Eddie.

The pen
is mightier
than the...

pigs

Where there's smoke there's...

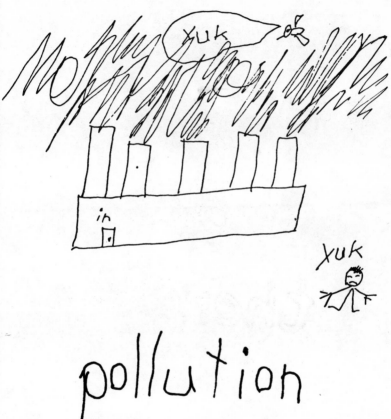

pollution